Pete's Bad Day

Written by Lucy Floyd
Illustrated by Abby Carter

A boy named Pete got up one day and found that things weren't going his way.

3

Pete slid off his bed and onto his feet.
He got messed up in his pillow and sheet.

4

So Pete screamed.

Pete put on jeans, but the jeans weren't right.
And his old green shirt felt much too tight.

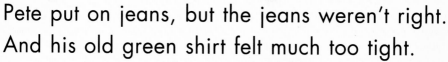

So Pete screamed.

Pete put on sneakers--can you guess?
The left on the right, oh, WHAT a mess!

8

So Pete screamed.

"Oh, Pete," said Mom, "will you please eat?
Why is your toast down on your feet?"

So Pete screamed.

He got his bike and hopped on the seat
but found no place to put his feet.

So Pete screamed.

13

"Okay," he said. "I'll start again. I'll sit right here and count to ten."

"That's IT!" Pete said. "Hear what I say.
I will not scream once more today."

"I know what to do. There is a way. I'll get back in bed and start a new day!"